Living Habitats

Heinemann InfoSearch

Living in a

Rain Forest

Heinemann Library
Chicago, Illinois

Carol Baldwin

Designed by Kimberly Saar, Heinemann Library
Illustrations and maps by John Fleck
Photo research by Alan Gottlieb
Printed and bound in the United States by Lake Book Manufacturing, Inc.

08 07 06 05 04
10 9 8 7 6 5 4 3 2 1

Library of Congress Cataloging-in-Publication Data
Baldwin, Carol, 1943-
  Living in a rain forest / Carol Baldwin.
     v. cm. -- (Living habitats)
Includes bibliographical references (p.   ).
Contents: What makes land a rain forest? -- Why are rain forests important? -- What's green and growing in the rain forest? -- What animals live in the rain forest? -- How do animals live in the rain forest? -- What's for dinner in the rain forest? -- How do rain forest animals get food? -- How does the rain forest affect people? -- How do people affect the rain forest.
  ISBN 1-4034-2992-8 (lib. bdg.) -- ISBN 1-4034-3234-1 (pbk.)
  1. Rain forests--Juvenile literature. [1. Rain forest ecology. 2. Rain forests. 3. Ecology.] I. Title.
  QH86.B36 2003
  577.34--dc21

2003001542

Acknowledgments
The author and publishers are grateful to the following for permission to reproduce copyright material:
p. 4 David Cavagnaro/Visuals Unlimited; p. 5 Charles Mauzy/Corbis; p. 6 Raymond Gehman/Corbis; p. 7 Michael & Patricia Fogden/Corbis; p. 9 Fritz Polking/Frank Lane Picture Agency/Corbis; p. 10 Wolfgang Kaehler/Corbis; p. 11 Bob Jensen/Bruce Coleman Inc.; p. 12 Gail M. Shumway/Bruce Coleman Inc.; p. 13 Stephen Dalton/Photo Researchers, Inc.; p. 14 Daniel Zupanc/Bruce Coleman Inc; p. 15 Charles V. Angelo/Photo Researchers, Inc.; p. 16T Art Wolf/Photo Researchers, Inc.; p. 16B Merlin D. Tuttle/Bat Conservation International; p. 17 David A. Northcott/Corbis; p. 18 John Giustina/Bruce Coleman Inc; p. 19 Tom Brakefield/Corbis; p. 20 Karen McGougan/Bruce Coleman Inc.; p. 21 Mark Newman/Photo Researchers, Inc.; p. 22 Wardene Weisser/Bruce Coleman Inc.; p. 24 George Holton/Photo Researchers, Inc.; p. 25 Jacques Jangoux/Stone/Getty Images; p. 26 Bruce Coleman Inc.; p. 27 Ulrike Welsch/Photo Researchers, Inc.

Cover photograph by Mark Taylor/Warren Photographic/Bruce Coleman Inc.

About the cover: This is a tropical rain forest. Every minute, 64 acres of tropical rain forests are destroyed worldwide.

Every effort has been made to contact copyright holders of any material reproduced in this book. Any omissions will be rectified in subsequent printings if notice is given to the publisher.

Some words are shown in bold, **like this**. You can find out what they mean by looking in the glossary.

Contents

What Makes Land a Rain Forest?

A rain forest, like all forests, is a large area covered with trees that grow close together. The leaves shade the ground. But rain forests are always wet. They get at least 80 inches (200 centimeters) of rain each year. Some get as much as 400 inches (1,000 centimeters).

Rainforests can be hot or cool

Tropical rain forests are found near the equator. They grow in more than 50 countries. Brazil, Indonesia, and Colombia have the largest rain forests. Temperatures are usually between 70 °F (21 °C) and 85 °F (29 °C) all year long. It does not cool down much at night. Much of the rain that falls **evaporates,** or changes to water vapor. This makes the air in a rain forest feel damp.

Water vapor in the air returns to the tropical rain forest as rainfall.

Temperate rain forests have lots of plants. But they don't have as many different **species** as tropical rain forests.

Temperate rain forests are not near the equator. They grow on the western edges of North and South America and in New Zealand and Tasmania. Here, damp ocean air brings between 80 and 200 inches (200 and 500 centimeters) of rain each year. These forests are warm in summer and cool in winter.

Rain forest soils differ

In tropical rain forests, the wet forest floor and warm temperatures make leaves on the ground rot fast. Any **nutrients** from dead plants, and even dead animals, that are released get used right away by living plants. Only the top few inches of soil in a tropical rain forest have enough nutrients to be **fertile.** The heavy rains also wash away **minerals** and other nutrients.

In temperate rain forests, the temperature is cooler. The dead plants on the ground rot slower and return minerals to the soil. So soil in temperate rain forests is fertile.

5

2 Why Are Rain Forests Important?

Rain forests contain many of the world's **species** of plants and animals. People live in rain forests and we all use things that come from the forests.

People live in rain forests

Mayans live in Central American rain forests. Many groups of Indians live in the rain forests of South America. Other rain forest people such as the Efe and Huli live in Africa and Indonesia. All these people depend on the rain forest for food, clothing, and homes.

Rain forests have many resources

Many foods come from plants that grow in rain forests. These include chocolate, bananas, and nuts. Many medicines also come from rain forest plants. Medicine from the rosy periwinkle is used to treat the blood disease leukemia.

Rain forest trees produce woods such as teak and cedar. Rubber comes from rain forest trees. So do coconut and palm oils. Other plants give us fibers used to make furniture and rugs.

> Many houseplants that people grow indoors are found in tropical rain forests.

Brightly colored arrow-poison frogs live in the rain forests of Central and South America. Some species have poison strong enough to kill a person.

Rain forests help Earth's climate

Trees and plants in rain forests clean the air, stop soil from washing away, and store water. They help balance Earth's water, air, and **climate.** Plants take carbon dioxide gas from the air and add oxygen. By removing carbon dioxide, plants help keep Earth's climates from becoming too warm.

Rain forests are home to many living things

Rain forests contain more species of plants and animals than any other **habitat** on Earth. The rain forests of Malaysia have 2,500 species of trees. Thousands of species of insects live in rain forests. As many as sixty different species of ants have been found in one rain forest tree. Many kinds of birds, snakes, and frogs also live in rain forests. Hundreds of species of **mammals** live in rain forests. These include jaguars, monkeys, and bears.

3 What's Green and Growing in a Rain Forest?

Plants in **tropical** rain forests grow in layers. A rain forest has three layers.

The canopy

The top layer of the rain forest is the **canopy.** It is made of the tops of tall trees. A few trees grow taller than the rest. These trees, called **emergents,** are about 100 to 120 feet (30 to 37 meters) tall. Another group of canopy trees are about 60 to 80 feet (18 to 24 meters) tall.

Canopy trees are **evergreens.** That means they don't lose all their leaves at the same time. Tropical rain forest trees, such as Brazil nut and mahogany trees, have wide leaves. These leaves block most of the sunlight. Only a tiny amount of sunlight filters down through the canopy.

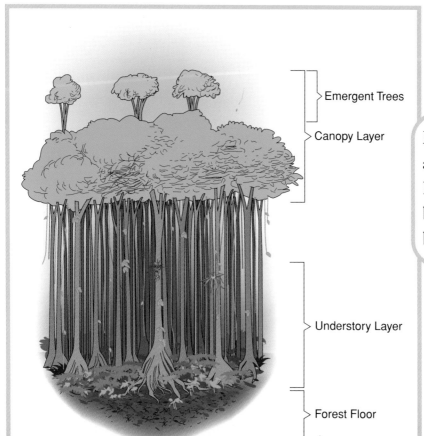

Emergent Trees

Canopy Layer

Understory Layer

Forest Floor

Emergent trees get a lot of sunlight. But they also get blown a lot more by the wind.

Most trees in tropical rain forests have shallow roots. Many trees have thick, finlike buttresses at the bottom of their trunks. Others have long stilt roots around their trunks. Tropical rain forest trees have very thin bark. The bark is only as thick as 6 to 10 sheets of paper.

In **temperate** rain forests, the canopy trees are **conifers** like fir, spruce, and cedar. These trees have needlelike leaves and make seeds in cones. They can grow more than 250 feet (76 meters) tall.

A strangler fig is parasitic, and the tree it grows on dies.

Epiphytes and strangler figs

Epiphytes grow on other plants. Their roots take in moisture from the damp air. Most grow high on canopy trees to get sunlight. Orchids and bromeliads are epiphytes. Epiphytes are helped by growing on trees, but the trees are not harmed. We say the epiphytes are commensal on trees. The trees are called the hosts.

A strangler fig starts life as an epiphyte. Its seed sprouts on the branch of a tree. The long roots grow down the trunk into the ground. The roots branch out and thicken. They surround the tree like a cage. Leaves on the fig block light from the tree's leaves. The tree finally dies and rots away. The "inside" of a strangler fig is empty.

9

The understory

The second layer, the **understory** is made of bushes and small trees that are **adapted** to grow in the shade. Some understory trees will quickly grow to take the place of a **canopy** a tree that falls. Other trees always stay small. They have large leaves that may help them gather sunlight in the dim light. Vines, such as **tropical** lianas, often grow up trees to reach sunlight.

The forest floor

Ferns, a few flowering plants, and mosses grow on the dim forest floor. Some vines grow along the floor toward patches of sunlight.

Fungi are not plants. They are living things that grow well in warm, dark, and damp places. Many different kinds of fungi, such as mushrooms, grow on the floor of tropical and **temperate** rain forests.

These mushrooms grow in temperate rain forests of North America.

What Animals Live in a Rain Forest?

The goliath beetle is one of the biggest of all insects. This African beetle can be five inches (almost 13 centimeters) long.

Rain forests are home to many different kinds of animals. About half of Earth's animal **species** live in tropical rain forests.

Insects and Spiders ✓

Insects make up the largest group of animals that live in rain forests. They include butterflies, beetles, many kinds of ants, and unusual insects like the stick insects. These look like twigs.

Many spiders, both large and small, live in rain forests. The Goliath bird-eating spider is a type of tarantula. It's about 11 inches (28 centimeters) across. That's as big as a dinner plate.

Fungus farmers

Leaf-cutter ants climb trees up to 100 feet (30 meters) tall and cut out small pieces of leaves. They carry the pieces to the forest floor and bury them underground. The leaves and saliva from the ants allow a kind of **fungus** to grow. This fungus is the only food the ants eat.

Amphibians and Reptiles

Rain forests are good places for **amphibians** like frogs, toads, and salamanders. They need a damp **habitat** and they lay their eggs in water.

Some frogs lay their eggs in water that collects between the leaves of bromeliads. Wallace's flying frog glides from tree to tree. Its large webbed feet and skin flaps on its front legs act like a parachute. It can travel as far as 24 feet (7.5 meters) through the air.

Many kinds of **reptiles** also live in rain forests. **Tropical** rainforest snakes include boas, pythons, vipers, and cobras. Lizards include iguanas, geckos, and chameleons.

Wallace's flying frog lives in the tropical rain forests of Sumatra and Borneo in Asia.

? Did you know?

The Choco Indians of South America rub darts for their blowguns across the backs of arrow-poison frogs. Hunters then shoot animals, such as monkeys, with the darts. The animals die quickly before they can escape into the forest.

Fish

Many different kinds of fish live in rivers and lakes in rain forests. At least twenty different **species** of piranhas live in lakes and rivers in Central and South America. Relatives of the piranha also live in Africa. Glass catfish live in Malaysia and Indonesia. Their skin is clear, like glass. You can even see their bones and body organs. Fish, such as salmon and trout, live in rivers of **temperate** rain forests.

An archer fish can leap 12 inches (30 centimeters) out of the water and catch an insect in its mouth.

Archer fish

Archer fish live in rivers in the rain forests of Africa, Southeast Asia, and Australia. A 10-inch (25-centimeter) archer fish can shoot a jet of water out of its mouth. It does this to knock down bugs flying or walking on plants above the water. They have been seen knocking down small insects up to 6 feet (2 meters) above the water's surface.

13

Birds

Rain forest birds vary greatly in size. The bee hummingbird is the world's smallest bird. It's only about 2 inches (5 centimeters) long, including its beak and tail. It weighs about as much as two paper clips. The world's largest eagle is the harpy eagle. It has a wingspan of 7 feet (2.1 meters). Both live in the **tropical** rain forests of Central and South America.

Many tropical rain forest birds, like parrots, macaws, and lorikeets, are very colorful. The Indian peacock has a long, colorful tail. It can be fanned out to attract a female. Most birds of paradise live in the rain forests of New Guinea. Many have long, strangely shaped feathers on their heads or tails.

These colorful parrots live in the rain forests of Australia and Indonesia. The female is bright red with a blue belly. The male has mostly green feathers.

? ## Did you know?

Pitohuis live in New Guinea. They are the first birds found to be poisonous. In 1991, scientists discovered that their skin and feathers contain a poison similar to that of arrow-poison frogs.

Spotted owls, pileated woodpeckers, and blue grouse are some of the birds that live in the **temperate** rain forests of North America.

Mammals

Mammals of many different shapes and sizes live in rain forests. Large cats, such as jaguars and tigers, usually live and hunt alone. Monkeys, chimpanzees, and gorillas live in groups. They move about and feed together. Orangutans are large apes that live alone. Hoofed rain forest mammals include tapirs, Sumatran rhinoceroses, and antelopes. The animals feed on rain forest plants. Tapirs are often found munching on water plants along rivers.

Bongos are the largest rain forest antelope.

 Did you know?

Unlike pet cats, tigers like to be near water. They are good swimmers and will go swimming to cool off on a hot day.

15

5 How Do Animals Live in a Rain Forest?

In any **habitat** animals need a place to live and food to eat. They also need to avoid enemies and find mates. Different rain forest animals have different ways of meeting their needs.

Some animals stay in one layer

Some animals always stay in the **canopy.** The canopy gives toucans and parrots safe nesting places. There they also find food, such as fruits and nuts. Sloths use their long claws to slowly move through the branches of canopy trees.

> Sloths eat, sleep, mate, and even give birth while hanging upside down in trees.

Some animals stay in the **understory.** Pacific tree frogs live on low growing trees in the **temperate** rain forest.

Many rain forest animals stay on the forest floor. Tapirs, deer, arrow-poison frogs, giant millipedes, and Gaboon vipers live on the forest floor.

> Honduran white bats, also called tent-making bats, sleep under leaves. They bite the leaf veins that attach to the central stalk so that the leaf droops over them. This is a flash photograph. In natural light, their white fur looks green from the light coming through the leaf. They are about 1 1/2 inches (a little less than 4 centimeters) long.

Some animals move from layer to layer

Some **nocturnal** fruit bats roost in understory trees during day. At night they fly to the canopy to feed on flower nectar and fruit. **Diurnal** ring-tailed lemurs live in groups. At night they share a canopy tree for sleeping. During the day, they move to the ground to feed on plants.

Martens, who live in temperate rain forests search for food, such as birds, mice, and fish, in trees or on the ground. They have their young in holes in the trees or in hollow logs on the ground.

The Indian fruit bat has a wing span of 4 feet (a little more than 1 meter). It finds ripe fruit with its sense of smell.

Boas are large snakes that move between the forest floor and the canopy searching for food. Morpho butterflies feed on nectar in canopy flowers. But they also feed on the juices of fallen fruit on the forest floor.

Animals have different eating habits

Some **species** that live together in the same level eat only one type of food. So koalas eat eucalyptus leaves, while sugar gliders feed on the trees' sap.

Others animals feed only in one layer of the rain forest. Antwrens are small birds that live in South American rain forests. There are several species of antwrens. But each one feeds in a different level of the forest. That way they can all find enough food.

Still other animals feed only during certain times. Colobus monkeys and small **mammals** called pottos live in the rain forests of western Africa. Both these species feed on fruit. Pottos are **nocturnal** and feed only at night. They use their keen noses and eyes to find food in the dark. Monkeys, however, are **diurnal** and feed only during the day.

A stong-smelling oil in the leaves they eat make koalas smell like some kinds of cough drops.

Many animals use sounds

It's hard for animals to communicate in the rain forest. Huge leaves and dim light in the **understory** and the forest floor make it hard to see one another. So, many animals use sounds.

Sounds let animals warn others of danger. Some monkeys even have different warning calls. They use one call for a snake, another for an eagle, and another for a leopard. Sounds help animals find a mate. Male frogs and birds call to attract females. Some animals also use sounds to keep other animals away. Jaguars roar to warn other jaguars to stay out of their territory.

Howler monkeys call to warn other groups of howler monkeys to stay out of their territory.

❓ Did you know?

Howler monkeys live in the rain forests of South America. Their calls are so loud they can be heard up to 3 miles (5 kilometers) away.

6 What's for Dinner in a Rain Forest?

All living things need food. Some living things, like plants, can make their own food. But animals need to find and eat food to live.

Plants

Plants make, or produce, their own food. So they are called **producers.** Plants like trees, vines, ferns, and mosses are rain forest producers. To make food, plants use carbon dioxide gas from the air. They also use water their roots take in from the ground. Plants need energy to change the carbon dioxide and water into sugars. The energy comes from sunlight. This process is called **photosynthesis.**

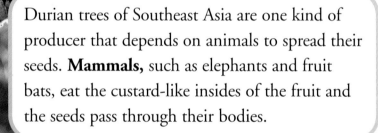

Durian trees of Southeast Asia are one kind of producer that depends on animals to spread their seeds. **Mammals,** such as elephants and fruit bats, eat the custard-like insides of the fruit and the seeds pass through their bodies.

Many plants need animals to spread their seeds so new plants can grow. Animals eat the fruits of plants. The seeds pass through the animals' bodies and are deposited at other places in the forest. Some plants depend on only one kind of animal to spread their seeds. If the animal becomes **extinct,** so will the plant.

Tree kangaroos live in the rain forests of northeastern Australia. These **herbivores** eat only tree leaves and fruit.

Animals

Animals are called **consumers** because they eat, or consume, food. Some animals, such as sloths, tapirs, and Asian elephants, eat only plants. These animals are called herbivores. Other animals, such as howler monkeys and birds of paradise, eat both plants and animals. They are called **omnivores.** Still others, such as harpy eagles and jaguars, eat only animals. They are **carnivores.**

The clean-up crew

Other kinds of consumers feed on dead plants and animals. They are called **decomposers. Bacteria, molds,** and some kinds of beetles are decomposers. Without them, dead plants and animals would pile up everywhere. The rain forest floor would be covered with them. Decomposers break down **nutrients** stored in dead plants and animals. They put them back into the soil, air, and water. Plants use the nutrients to help them grow.

7 How Do Rain Forest Animals Get Food?

Some animals hunt other animals. Other animals **forage** or **scavenge.**

Hunting

Animals that hunt and kill other animals for food are **predators.** Harpy eagles are predators. They hunt and eat monkeys and sloths. Diana monkeys eat mainly plants. But they also hunt and eat insects and young birds. So sometimes they are predators. Animals that predators eat are **prey.** Sloths are the prey of harpy eagles.

Some rain forest animals are both predators and prey. Squirrel monkeys eat insects, spiders, young birds, fruits, and nuts. They are predators. However, squirrel monkeys are also eaten by harpy eagles. So, they are also prey.

Foragers

Some animals, such as tapirs, antelopes, and wild pigs are **foragers.** They move about searching for food. They are often found along river banks where they find plenty of tender leaves near the ground.

The harpy eagle flies from tree to tree looking for food.

Scavenging

King vultures are rain forest **scavengers.** Scavengers are animals that eat the bodies of animals that are already dead. Wood lice are also scavengers. They feed on tiny dead creatures and rotting plants.

Planning the menu

The path that shows who eats what is a **food chain.** All living things are parts of food chains. In the **temperate** rain forest, small micelike animals called voles feed on plants. Owls eat the voles.

Another temperate rain forest food chain includes deer that feed on leaves and fruits. Deer are eaten by cougars. All the food chains that are connected in a **habitat** make up a **food web.**

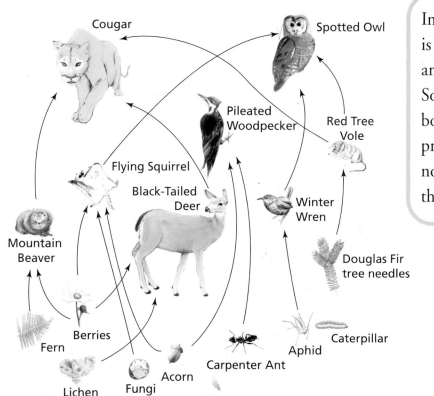

Cougar

Spotted Owl

Pileated Woodpecker

Red Tree Vole

Flying Squirrel

Black-Tailed Deer

Winter Wren

Mountain Beaver

Douglas Fir tree needles

Berries

Caterpillar

Fern

Aphid

Carpenter Ant

Lichen   Fungi   Acorn

In a food web, an arrow is drawn from "dinner" and points to the "diner." So, producers are on the bottom of the web. "Top" predators, animals that no one else eats, are at the top.

23

How Does a Rain Forest Affect People?

Some rain forest people hunt and gather

The Efe people live in the Ituri rain forest in Africa. They are a tribe of honey gatherers. They get help from a bird called the greater honeyguide. It leads the Efe to trees that have bees' nests. The Efe climb the tree with a bundle of smoking leaves. The smoke puts the bees to sleep. The Efe gather the honey. They leave the beeswax behind as food for the bird. The Efe also gather fruits and hunt animals in the forest. They take only what they need and move on. So they don't harm the rain forest.

The Efe men and boys hunt with bows and arrows. The women and girls search for nuts, berries, mushrooms, and roots.

Flood waters bring **nutrients** to the soil along the rivers. This allows farmers to grow crops for food.

Some rain forest people farm along rivers

In the South American rain forest, most people live along rivers that **flood** every year. They build small homes on tall poles to stay above flood waters. Floods make soil near the river **fertile** enough to grow crops every year. People grow corn and **manioc.** Crops are planted and grown when the water is low. People also hunt in the forest and fish in the river. When the water rises, people use boats to get around.

? Did you know?

In **tropical** rain forests, some mosquitoes carry the organisms that cause the disease malaria. People catch malaria from mosquito bites. More than one million people die each year from malaria. The drug quinine is used to treat malaria. It comes from the cinchona tree that grows in tropical rain forests.

How Do People Affect a Rain Forest?

The rain forest **habitat** may be the most valuable land on Earth. People affect the rain forest in many ways.

People destroy rain forests

Every second, more than one acre of rain forest is lost. Poor farmers cut and burn trees to grow food. Ranchers cut forests to make pastures for cattle. Loggers cut trees for wood. Food companies cut forests to make huge farms that grow foods like coffee or bananas.

When trees are cut, plants, animals, and native peoples lose their homes. Many become **extinct.** Without trees, rain washes away soil. Soil that is left is not **fertile** enough to regrow the forests. Soil washing into rivers can damage that habitat, too. Fewer trees and burning those that are cut mean more carbon dioxide in the air. This can affect Earth's **climate.**

Cutting all the trees in part of a rain forest is called clear-cutting.

People mine in rain forests

Many rain forests contain large deposits of **minerals,** such as gold, nickel, and iron. Mines dug to reach the minerals are big, open pits. Roads and railroads built through the forest carry the minerals out. Large areas of habitat are lost. **Pollution** from mining poisons rivers. Rain forest people who eat river fish may become sick.

People work to protect forest

All over the world, people are trying to protect and save the rain forests. Around the world, large areas of rain forest have been turned into national parks. In many of these parks, logging and mining aren't allowed.

People visiting this rain forest in Peru see the canopy close-up from cable cars high above the ground.

Ecotourism is also helping protect rain forests. People come to learn about the plants and animals. Tourists pay local people to act as guides. Ecotourism helps local people earn money, while the habitat is protected.

27

Fact File

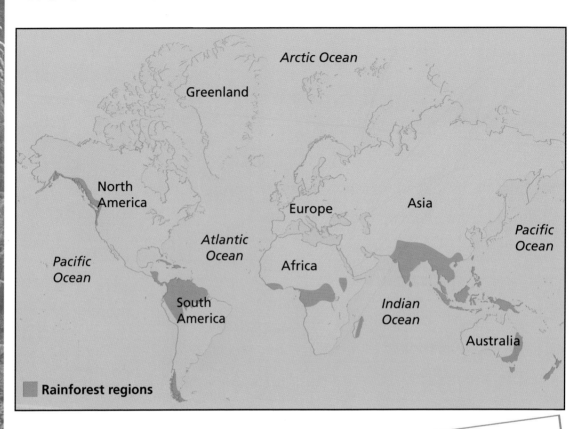

Arctic Ocean

Greenland

North America

Europe

Asia

Pacific Ocean

Atlantic Ocean

Pacific Ocean

Africa

South America

Indian Ocean

Australia

Rainforest regions

The World Heritage List

UNESCO, the United Nations Educational, Scientific, and Cultural Organization, adopted the World Heritage Treaty in 1972, and more than 160 nations have signed it. A committee produces the World Heritage List. It contains more than 700 human-built, **cultural,** and natural sites in the world. About 140 of them are natural areas, including rain forests. Funding is provided to help countries protect their sites. Sites on the list must have "outstanding universal value from the point of view of science, conservation, or natural beauty." Olympic National Park in Washington, which has a temperate rain forest, is a World Heritage Site.

Earth's Rain Forests

Country/area	Original amount of rain forest (square miles)	Present amount of rain forest (square miles)	Amount of rain forest lost each year (square miles)	Year when rain forest could be gone
Bolivia	35,000	17,000	580	2031
Brazil	1,100,000	695,000	19,000	2039
Central America	193,000	21,000	1,300	2018
Columbia	270,000	69,000	2,500	2117
Congo	39,000	31,000	270	2016
Ecuador	51,000	17,000	1,200	2016
Indonesia	471,000	205,000	4,600	2047
Cote D'Ivoire	62,000	1,500	965	2004
Laos	42,000	9,700	390	2027
Madagascar	24,000	3,900	770	2007
Mexico	154,000	42,000	2,700	2018
Nigeria	28,000	3,900	1,500	2005
Philippines	96,000	3,000	1,000	2005
Thailand	168,000	8,500	2,300	2006

Glossary

adapted changed to live under certain conditions

amphibian animal with a moist skin that lives on land but lays its eggs in water. Frogs, toads, and salamanders are amphibians.

bacteria living things too small to be seen except with a microscope. Some bacteria are decomposers.

canopy layer of the rain forest made of the tops of tall trees

carnivore animal that eats only other animals

climate average weather conditions in an area over a long period of time

conifer tree or shrub that has needlelike leaves that stay green and remain on the tree all year. They produce their seeds in cones.

consumer living thing that needs plants for food

cultural something about the people who live in an area, including their tools, homes, and art

decomposer living thing that breaks down the bodies of dead plants and animals. This puts nutrients from dead plants and animals back into the soil, air, and water.

diurnal active during the day

ecotourism travel to a natural habitat to see and learn about it

emergent rain forest tree that grows taller than the rest of the trees

epiphyte plant that grows on other plants for support, but gets nutrients from the air and rain

evaporate change from a liquid to a gas

evergreen having green leaves all year long

extinct no longer existing on Earth

fertile able to grow plants easily

flood great flow of water over what is usually dry land

food chain path that shows who eats what in a habitat

food web group of connected food chains in a habitat

forage to wander about in search of food

forager animal or person that wanders about in search of food

fungus (plural: **fungi**) living thing that feeds on dead or living plant or animal matter. Mushrooms and molds are fungi.

habitat place where a plant or animal lives

herbivore animal that eats only plants

mammal warm-blooded animal that breathes with lungs, has a bony skeleton, has hair or fur, and produces milk to feed its young

manioc tropical plant that is used to make a kind of flour

mineral any material dug from the earth by mining; nutrient needed in small amounts for the growth of a plant or animal. Gold, iron, and diamonds are mined minerals. Iron, calcium, and phosphates are nutrient minerals.

mold living thing that uses dead plants and animals for food. Molds are decomposers.

nocturnal active at night

nutrient material that is needed for the growth of a plant or animal

omnivore animal that eats plants and animals

photosynthesis process by which green plants trap the sun's energy and use it to change carbon dioxide and water into sugars

pollution harmful materials in the water, air, or land

predator animal that hunts and eats other animals

prey animal that is hunted and eaten by other animals

producer living thing that can use sunlight to make its own food

reptile land animal with a scaly skin. Snakes, lizards, turtles, and crocodiles are reptiles.

scavenge to feed on the bodies of dead animals

scavenger animal that eats the bodies of animals that are already dead

species group of organisms that are enough alike that they can mate and produce offspring

temperate region that has a warm summer and a cool winter

tropical region near the equator that is warm to hot all year round

understory rain forest layer formed by bushes, young trees, and vines

More Books to Read

Castner, James L. *Surviving in the Rain Forest.* New York: Benchmark Books, 2002.

Doris, Ellen. *Life at the Top: Discoveries in a Tropical Forest Canopy.* Austin, Tex.: Raintree/Steck-Vaughn, 2000.

Fowler, Allan. *Living in a Rain Forest.* Danbury, Conn.: Children's Press, 2000.

Macken, JoAnn Early. *Rain Forest Animals.* Milwaukee, Wisc.: Gareth Stevens Pubishers., 2002.

Pirotta, Saviour. *Predators in the Rain Forest.* Austin, Tex.: Raintree/Steck-Vaughn, 1999.

Telford, Carole and Rod Theodorou. *Up a Rainforest Tree.* Chicago: Heinemann Library, 1998.

Index